FEB - 8 2017

P9-DNF-795

TRANSGENDER PIONEERS

LANA
WACHOWSKI

JEFF MAPUA

ROSEN
PUBLISHING

NEW YORK

Published in 2017 by The Rosen Publishing Group, Inc.
29 East 21st Street, New York, NY 10010

Copyright © 2017 by The Rosen Publishing Group, Inc.

First Edition

All rights reserved. No part of this book may be reproduced in any form without permission in writing from the publisher, except by a reviewer.

Library of Congress Cataloging-in-Publication Data

Names: Mapua, Jeff, author.
Title: Lana Wachowski / Jeff Mapua.
Description: First edition. | New York : Rosen Publishing Group, Inc., 2017. | Series: Transgender pioneers | Includes bibliographical references and index.
Identifiers: LCCN 2015047610 | ISBN 9781508171607 (library bound)
Subjects: LCSH: Wachowski, Lana, 1965—Juvenile literature. | Transsexuals—United States—Biography—Juvenile literature. | Transgender people—United States—Biography—Juvenile literature. | Motion picture producers and directors—United States—Biography—Juvenile literature.
Classification: LCC HQ77.8.W33 M37 2017 | DDC 306.76/8092—dc23
LC record available at http://lccn.loc.gov/2015047610

Manufactured in China

CONTENTS

Lana Wachowski (left) pictured with her sister and professional partner Lilly (formerly known as Andy, right) at the Los Angeles premiere of their film *Cloud Atlas* on October 24, 2012.

Lana Wachowski never wanted the spotlight. From her days as a bright student to her career as a big-budget Hollywood film director, she always shied away from the attention that her hard work merited. Her privacy was vitally important to her, and once famous, she strove to keep her personal life out of the media despite being in a profession in which the public craves personal drama to fill headlines and entertainment news shows. However, there was one thing about herself that Wachowski felt was even more important than her hard-fought anonymity, and she was willing to sacrifice her privacy in order to fight for it.

Lana Wachowski is a transgender, or trans, woman. At birth, she was assigned male, but internally she identified as female. As a child, Lana's gender identity caused her to feel confused, and it resulted in a difficult youth. As

3 0053 01252 5708

an adult, Wachowski has forgone her anonymity and stepped out into the spotlight to share her story in hopes that other transgender individuals will not have to suffer the same feelings of confusion, isolation, and depression that she did growing up.

There are many brave individuals in the transgender community who take the courageous step of coming out publicly. Wachowski, however, had the unique position of also being a successful Hollywood director with several multi-million dollar movies in her filmography. In 1999, her first major box-office hit was *The Matrix,* an action-packed movie that she directed with her sister and professional partner, Lilly Wachowski. Audiences around the world were wowed by its futuristic style, relatable heroes, and crisp fight choreography. The Wachowskis infused their love of philosophy into the film, which, in turn, spawned multiple academic studies and philosophical debates. The success propelled Lana and her sister into rarefied air. However, despite their success and the fame that it brought, the Wachowskis maintained their privacy and declined all interviews and public appearances for several years.

When she felt ready, Lana Wachowski came out as trans to her close friends and family. Their response was uplifting and humbling, particularly how easily her parents embraced their daughter. Wachowski was able to find the support that she needed in her family. (Years later, her sister Lilly also came out as transgender and transitioned from male to female.) Lana was also able to find love and get married. But while she was lucky, Wachowski knew that there were others not as blessed with good fortune and understanding families. She read about victims of intolerance and hate crimes such as Gwen Araujo, a transgender woman who, in 2002, was murdered by four men because she was a trans woman. Wachowski knew that while her family had been accepting, much prejudice and ignorance still existed in the world around her.

Many of the Wachowskis' films deal with heroes who face overwhelming odds to break the status quo and overcome villains who hold power and use it to terrorize or oppress others. In her personal life, Lana Wachowski took the path of the hero and spoke out against the prejudice, ignorance, and intolerance that oppress the transgender community. She sacrificed something she held dear—her privacy—to fight for a greater good. Wachowski's honesty and willingness to share her experience have positively impacted lives around the world.

CHAPTER 1

EARLY LIFE

Before stepping behind the lens of a camera, Lana Wachowski was just like any other kid growing up in 1960s Chicago. She shared the same interests as many other children her age. Lana enjoyed playing games with her siblings and watching movies with her parents. However, even in her youth, Lana began to feel that something was different about her. She had trouble finding the right words to describe exactly what it was. In retrospect, Wachowski came to understand that what she was experiencing was gender dysphoria—the unhappiness produced by an incongruity between one's gender identity (the gender that a person internally feels that they are) and their apparent physical sex (the physical traits with which they were born).

FAMILY LIFE

Lana Wachowski was born on June 21, 1965, in Chicago, Illinois, to Ron and Lynne Wachowski. Lana was designated male at birth, and her parents named her Laurence (or Larry, for short). Ron owned a machinery-importing business. Lynne had a career as a nurse before becoming an expressionist painter. Lana has three sisters, including Lilly, her professional partner.

The Wachowskis were a close-knit family and lived in Beverly, a middle-class neighborhood on the South Side of Chicago. Lana's parents were protective of their children, and Lana also had a special protector in Lilly, who always watched out for her. This particular family trait would be of the utmost importance later in life as Lana struggled with her identity. Coming out as transgender can be a daunting task, and having family support is lucky and invaluable—an advantage that many members of the transgender community do not have. After her transition, Lana compared having parents like hers to winning the lottery.

Lana's relationship with her sister, Lilly, was always very close. As directors, their working relationship reaped the benefits of their lifelong bond. Their father, Ron, said that, as children,

A NOTE ABOUT LANGUAGE

Just as transgender rights evolve over time and our culture becomes more aware of the issues that affect members of the transgender community, so, too, must the language we use evolve to reflect these changes. *Cisgender* is a term that serves as the antonym of *transgender*. A cisgender individual is a person who identifies as the gender that they were assigned at birth. The related concept of *cisnormativity* refers to the common perception or use of language that implies that all people are inherently cisgender and that transgender individuals are a deviation from a perceived norm. This assumption is incorrect and highly offensive to members of the transgender community.

Much of the language that we use can be unconsciously cisnormative. Transgender rights activists advocate against the use of gender binary–enforcing constructions or terms such as "he or she" or "him- or herself" to refer to hypothetical or unidentified individuals. Instead, the use of gender-neutral pronouns such as "they," "them," and "themself" is recommended instead. Furthermore, a trans individual should always be referred to by their chosen name and gender pronouns—even when discussing their life prior to transition. Therefore, we refer to Lana by her chosen name and with female pronouns ("she," "her," and "herself"), even when discussing her childhood and adult life prior to transition. When in doubt, always ask a transgender person which pronouns they prefer. If you cannot ask, use gender-neutral pronouns (such as "they") or pronouns consistent with their appearance and gender expression.

they were inseparable. In a September 2012 article for *The New Yorker*, Ron recalled that Lana "would come up with a crazy idea to hang ropes from a tree and make a swing or trapeze, and [Lilly] would be the person to grab hold of the rope, climb, and crash down."

Years later, as the pair were directing one of their first films, their working relationship could be described as almost telepathic. The two would not need to speak to each other to know what the other was thinking. "They have the same picture in their mind without talking. I watched two bodies and one brain," Ron recalled. Australian director James McTeigue, who worked with the duo on several projects, echoed this sentiment in the same *New Yorker* article. He said, "There's a little bit of myth in it. The unification of mind comes through the filmmaking."

Lana, the older of the two siblings, is more talkative. People describe Lilly as the tougher sibling, while Lana, in contrast, loves to talk about philosophy. The two often defer to one another, and they shared a love of comic books and *The Lord of the Rings* trilogy in their youth. They would spend weekends in their attic playing the popular role-playing game Dungeons & Dragons, only making appearances to refuel their bodies with whatever was in the fridge downstairs. Their creativity and enthusiasm for telling stories were blossoming. Along with their

While growing up, Lana and Lilly Wachowski shared many common interests, including a love of the role-playing game Dungeons & Dragons (shown here).

friends, the two created a game of their own, with a three-hundred-page manual, and named it *High Adventure.*

A CONFUSING TIME

Whatever comforts Lana found at home, she would have trouble finding any at school and in the outside world. Lana's gender dysphoria meant that she often felt stuck between genders, something that made growing up a confusing time. As a result, she struggled with depression and suicidal thoughts. Many transgender individuals have trouble expressing their gender identity when they are young. Because of her assigned male gender, Lana felt unable to express her true gender identity as a female through behavior, clothing, and hairstyle. Lana, and many other transgender youth, often fear bullying, punishment, or negative attention if they express their gender identity.

TROUBLE IN SCHOOL

As a child, Lana transferred from a public school to a private Catholic school. Some of her school's rules were rigid and limiting. Uniforms were required. Girls and boys stood in separate lines before class. While in public school, Lana had been allowed to play with other girls. She had also been allowed to keep her hair long. However, the Catholic school required Lana to get a short haircut. It was around this time that Lana understood her gender identity.

Wachowski later recalled what it was like to reconcile how she felt inside with what the school expected of her. "I have a formative memory of walking through the girls' line and hesitating, knowing that my clothes didn't match," Lana explained in a September 2012 interview with *The New Yorker*. The other line did not feel right to Lana, either, so one day, she just stopped between them. Lana said, "I was stuck—I couldn't move. I think some unconscious part of me figured I was exactly where I belonged: betwixt."

The nun that led the class became frustrated with Lana's inability to stand in the boys' line and refusal to explain herself. The nun began to hit her. Coincidentally (even Lana recognizes that the timing is movie perfect), Lana's mother, Lynne, happened to be driving by the school and witnessed the incident. She stepped in to protect her daughter. Later, at home, Lynne tried to get her daughter to explain what had happened to instigate such a reaction from the nun, but Lana was unable to find the right words to explain her inner struggle. In her October

2012 acceptance speech for the Human Rights Campaign's (HRC) Visibility Award, Lana recalled, "[My mother] tells me to look at her but I don't want to, because when I do I am unable to understand why she cannot see me."

Lana's inability to neatly fit in with the boys at her school—as she was expected to by her teachers and peers—made her a target for bullying. "As a result, I hid and found tremendous solace in books, vastly preferring imagined worlds to this world," Lana told *The New Yorker*.

Lana suffered through feelings of anxiety and isolation as well as insomnia and depression. When some male classmates began to grow facial hair, Lana was terrified of what she might see in the mirror. She did not have anyone to look to for help as a guide. Without an example or model to follow, she began to believe that she was "a freak…broken, that there [was] something wrong with [her], that [she would] never be lovable."

By her sophomore year of high school, Lana says she wasn't sleeping much. Her depression worsened. She did not feel like she belonged anywhere. In her acceptance speech for the HRC's Visibility Award, Lana narrated a suicide attempt she planned, but did not follow through on, that year.

LILA PERRY

On August 27, 2015, a group of parents in Hillsboro, Missouri, (near St. Louis) raised an issue to their school board. A transgender female student began using the girls' locker room at Hillsboro High School. The parents read their petition aloud, including a statement asking the school board to refrain from extending privileges to "confused teenagers who want to be something they are not sexually." The school board

On August 31, 2015, Lila Perry speaks to reporters about her decision to use the girls' locker room at her high school.

did not meet the parents' demands. The following Monday, a group of students organized a walkout during school with support from their parents. In response to the student walkout, Lila Perry, the seventeen-year-old transgender student, and her supporters organized their own rally.

"I am a girl. I am not going to be pushed away to another bathroom," said Lila Perry in an interview with CNN. Lila said that she was thirteen when she began to

feel that she did not identify as the gender that she was assigned at birth. So in her senior year, she began wearing skirts, makeup, and a longhaired wig. She also began using the girls' locker room. Anticipating that some students and parents might take issue with Lila's use of the girls' locker room, the school offered a single-occupancy bathroom as an alternative.

Lila Perry's situation highlights one town's struggles to adequately protect transgender teenagers' rights. The small town of less than three thousand people became the center of national attention as supporters and critics discussed Perry's decision to outwardly express her gender identity.

In a press conference statement, Perry offered herself as an example for transgender teens in similar positions across the country. "I believe that my school isn't special. I believe that there are places like Hillsboro all over the country where young people are hurting, feeling alone, and being discriminated against because of who they are. And I believe it's important, now that I've been put in this position, for me to stay strong for all of those young people and for my community."

CONNECTING WITH FILMMAKING

One of the joys that Lana did have growing up was going to the movies. The Wachowski family made frequent trips to see flicks at the local theater or drive-in. Ron and Lynne were film enthusiasts and took the family to any movie they found interesting, regardless of the movie's rating. In *The New Yorker*, Lilly Wachowski was quoted remembering, "We would have 'movie orgies'—double features, triple features, drive-ins. I was so young that I didn't know what the word 'orgy' meant, but I knew that, whatever it was, I liked it."

In line with her family's interest in film, Lana joined the theater club at her school. One of Lana's older sisters influenced her to join, but Lana was mostly interested in an old storeroom in the theater filled with costumes, dresses, shoes, and—perhaps most important—privacy. There, Lana was able to sit, read, and try on some of the clothes. Lana recalled a time when she was wearing a brocaded dress with a built-in corset in the secluded storeroom when the stage manager called for her. When the door swung open, Lana dove into the racks of dresses to hide what she was wearing. Her heart was "pounding like a mouse, listening to [the stage manager] call

[her] name over and over, praying that somehow [she] might remain invisible."

Beyond the stage and cinema, Lana's interest in comic books and Dungeons & Dragons—interests she shared with her closest sister, Lilly—helped her escape reality. Lana explained the appeal of Dungeons & Dragons (D&D, for short): "In D&D, you have nothing but your imagination. It asks all of the players to try to imagine the same space, the same image. This is very much the process of making a film." Lana and Lilly also created their own games that mixed various genres such as sci-fi, fantasy, and action. The games were a preview of the style that would later be incorporated into their films.

When Lana was ten years old and Lilly seven, their parents had them watch director Stanley Kubrick's highly influential film *2001: A Space Odyssey.* Lana did not immediately take to the movie. The film includes a strange black monolith that appears in various sequences. Its inclusion in the movie puzzled Lana. Her father, Ron, made it clearer when he explained that the monolith was a symbol. This was a major, transitional moment in Lana's life. "That simple sentence went into my brain and rearranged things in such an unbelievable way that I don't think I've been the same since.

Shown is a scene from Stanley Kubrick's *2001: A Space Odyssey*. The influential film inspired Lana to become a filmmaker.

Something clicked inside," Lana told *The New Yorker*. That movie was a major reason why Lana became a filmmaker.

It was also during this time that Lana and Lilly decided to direct together as a team. One of their earliest works was a cassette tape onto which they recorded a reading of a play inspired by *The Shadow*, a classic comic book and radio program. It was the first project in what would become a successful career in Hollywood for the siblings. But, like most things in Lana's early life, it would not be easy getting there.

CHAPTER 2

BREAKING INTO THE BUSINESS

With a love of movies and cinema firmly established, Lana and Lilly Wachowski set their minds to making their passion into a career. The road proved to be full of twists and turns, with dead ends testing their resolve to make their dreams a reality. The two tried their hands at higher education, various forms of writing, and labor-intensive jobs. They would need a little luck and a lot of hard work to get where they wanted to be.

BEFORE THEY WERE STARS

While a student at the Whitney M. Young Magnet High School, Lana learned the ropes in the school's television and theater programs. While in high school, Lana and Lilly painted superheroes on their aunt's garage door. To earn money for college, they parlayed this painting experience into starting a house-painting business.

The siblings saved what they could. Combining her portion of the money saved with a student loan, Lana headed for Bard College in upstate New York. However, the education was not what she hoped it would be, and the professors' credentials were not up to Lana's standards. "I thought the teachers had to be way smarter than me to justify the loan, but some of them hadn't read half the books I'd read," Lana said in a September 2012 interview with *The New Yorker*. Meanwhile, Lilly enrolled in classes at Emerson College in Boston, Massachusetts.

Disappointed with the education she was receiving, Lana dropped out of college and moved to Portland, Oregon. There, she wrote and worked on various projects including an adaptation of author William Goldman's *The Princess Bride*. Showing a bit of courage, Lana got ahold of Goldman's phone number and called him to ask for the rights. Goldman promptly hung up on her. In 1987, Goldman would adapt the novel for film himself.

Lilly's college experience was no better than Lana's. She dropped out of Emerson during her sophomore year and moved back to

Chicago. There, Lana reunited with her sister, and the two started another new business. This time it was a construction business, and the two learned most of their skills on the job. In one instance, they were able to land a project using only their convincing self-confidence, insisting that they were completely capable of building an elevator shaft. Their salesmanship was top notch even though they lacked previous experience building elevator shafts and plans on how to carry out the job.

No matter where their careers went, Lana and Lilly always maintained their interests in fantasy fiction, comic books, Japanese anime, and B-grade movies. They eventually landed a job together at one of the top comic book companies in the world.

COMICS AND *CARNIVORE*

The Wachowski sisters continued to work and write. They relied on their tenacity to land their dream job. In the early 1990s, Lana made a trip to New York with a plan to knock on the doors of comic-book publishers until someone opened the door and give her and her sister a chance. Her plan worked, and Lana was able to get herself and Lilly writing positions at the world famous Marvel Comics.

The series they wrote for was called *Ectokid*, drawn by artist Steve Skroce and created by filmmaker Clive Barker. It was a short-lived series that followed the adventures of fourteen-year old Dexter Mungo and his supernatural abilities.

Around this time, Lana married a woman named Thea Bloom. Thea and Lana signed a prenuptial agreement prior to their October 30, 1993, wedding. Like many personal aspects of her life, Lana has kept the details of this marriage very guarded and out of the public eye.

While Lana and Lilly had success both in construction as well as in the comic-book world, bigger things were in store for the duo. After college, Lana had learned about a B movie film director named Roger Corman. B movies are movies with low budgets generally considered low quality, and Roger Corman specialized in the genre. In 1990, Corman published his autobiography titled *How I Made a Hundred Movies in Hollywood and Never Lost a Dime*. Lana shared the book with Lilly, and the two decided to write their own Corman-style screenplay about cannibals. The duo's first script was called *Carnivore*.

Carnivore's plot was a twisted tale about a soup kitchen that feeds the poor an addictive stew with ingredients that included the chopped-up remains of the rich. The Wachowskis sent the script to ten addresses they had selected from an agent handbook. They received two offers from agents to represent them, including Lawrence Mattis, the agent who would go on to become their manager. Mattis wanted to sign the Wachowskis because they had "a surety to their writing that really popped."

Mattis may have enjoyed their writing, but in an April 1999 article in the *New York Times*, Lilly recalls a less enthusiastic response among Hollywood producers. In Lilly's words, "The script was too disturbing. We showed it to some

Lawrence Mattis (center) attends a film premiere at the Toronto International Film Festival on September 19, 2015.

people in Hollywood who said: 'This is a bad idea. I can't make this. I'm rich.'" Investors were scared away by the dark nature of *Carnivore*. The screenplay was never turned into a film. However, this rejection did not stop the Wachowskis. They would soon receive their first taste of success—and the trappings of the fame they so abhorred.

GETTING THEIR FOOT IN THE DOOR: *ASSASSINS* (1995)

Lana and Lilly's parents were supportive of their dreams and encouraged them to continue writing and creating. While the screenplay was not picked up to make a movie, *Carnivore* did help the siblings create a little buzz in the film industry. Movie studios began to take note of these talented new writers, and the Wachowskis were eventually granted a chance to write a screenplay that would ultimately make it to production.

That screenplay became the 1995 film *Assassins*, starring Sylvester Stallone, Antonio Banderas, and Julianne Moore. It was an action-packed story set in the world of hired killers. The screenplay was optioned, or entered into a contract to be made into a film, by film producer Dino De Laurentiis. At the same time the Wachowski siblings were renovating their par-

WENDY CARLOS

In 1969, an album called *Switched-on Bach* won a Grammy Award for its composer, Wendy Carlos. The album is credited with popularizing the Moog synthesizer and creating commercial outlets for electronic musical instruments. Before the album, electronic music was unpopular. But *Switched-on Bach* popularized electronic music and made it appeal to classical music fans. It became a bestseller, selling millions of copies.

While she had much success, Carlos was suffering internally. She was a trans woman but had not yet transitioned from male to female and, consequently, was experiencing gender dysphoria. While her gender dysphoria began in her youth, Carlos grew unhappier as the years wore on. As an adult, she contacted an expert on the medical treatment necessary to begin transitioning. Dr. Harry Benjamin was a German-born endocrinologist living in New York. Benjamin was well known for his work on transsexualism. Benjamin first prescribed a treatment of estrogen, hormones that promote the development of female physical characteristics. Carlos then underwent sex reassignment surgery (SRS), a doctor-supervised surgical intervention that some transgender people choose to undergo as part of their transition.

After her transition, Carlos continued to find great success in her musical career, composing scores for landmark films such as director Stanley Kubrick's *A Clockwork Orange* and *The Shining*, as well as Disney's

Wendy Carlos was a pioneer of electronic music and one of the first trans celebrities to transition publicly.

Tron. However, at the urging of her friends, who were concerned about the potential hardships her new identity would cause her career, she continued to work under the name she was given at birth, Walter Carlos.

For a time, Carlos went to great lengths to maintain her double identities. It was not uncommon for Wendy to wear a "Walter disguise," and she would travel to far-off locations to escape the public eye. Wendy eventually decided to come out publicly in the May 1979 issue of *Playboy* magazine. The response to her announcement came as a significant shock to her. "The public turned out to be amazingly tolerant or, if you wish, indifferent," she said in a July 1985 article for *People* magazine. "There had never been any need of this charade to have taken place. It had proven a monstrous waste of years of my life."

ents' house in Chicago. De Laurentiis had produced some of the biggest movies in Hollywood, each with mega budgets and big-name stars.

De Laurentiis wowed Lana and Lilly by entertaining the two with champagne and stories about celebrity actors. Lana and Lilly were introduced to the business side of filmmaking when De Laurentiis sold their screenplay for five times the amount he had paid. The director attached to the project was Richard

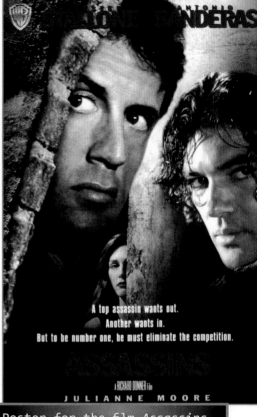

Poster for the film *Assassins* (1995)

Donner, who had a career filled with groundbreaking successes such as *The Goonies, Lethal Weapon,* and the memorable 1978 film *Superman.* The screenplay seemed to be headed toward certain success, with that type of talent onboard the project. However, that success was not to be.

The Wachowskis' original creative vision for the movie was compromised as other writers were brought on to make revisions to the screenplay. Lana recalled that these revisions included removing the Wachowskis' subtext and visual metaphors. The end product was so far removed from their creation that Lana and Lilly tried (but failed) to get their names taken off the credits.

Critics were not kind to the film. *Assassins* performed poorly at the box office and failed to earn back the money spent in production. It was only the fifty-ninth highest grossing movie of the year. The two budding filmmakers hated the end result. Their failure to distance themselves from the movie hardened their resolve to avoid

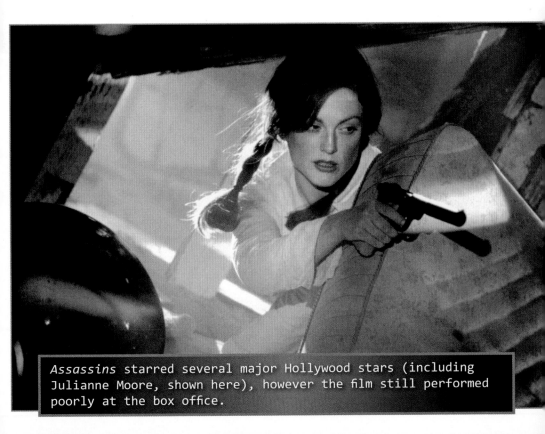

Assassins starred several major Hollywood stars (including Julianne Moore, shown here), however the film still performed poorly at the box office.

suffering through the same experience in the future. But this would prove to be just the beginning for Lana and Lilly's career. They finished the renovations on their parents' house, quit doing construction odd jobs, and dedicated themselves to being the filmmakers they always dreamed they would be.

DIRECTING *BOUND* (1996)

Lawrence Mattis recalls that in 1994, the Wachowskis were "the hot flavor of the month." The pair had been working on a new script for two years, one that they insisted on directing themselves. However, this new script was perhaps too strange and too much of a risk for their debut directorial effort. That script would turn out to be *The Matrix*. To prove that they were capable of making that film, they agreed to take on a smaller project called *Bound* first.

Lilly and Lana were able to move on from their disappointment with *Assassins* and make their directorial debut with *Bound*. The stylish and violent 1996 movie, starring Jennifer Tilly and Gina Gershon, was about two lesbian women who take off with a suitcase filled with millions of dollars. At the time of the film's production, viewers were not used to such prominent inclusion of LGBTQ characters in a crime thriller. Lilly

Poster for the film *Bound* (1996).

would later note that, "The fun is in bending and twisting convention."

Unfortunately, Lilly and Lana may have bent and twisted conventions too much for some viewers' liking in *Bound*. Test audiences walked out during the movie because of the graphic nature of some of the sequences, including one in which a character's finger is sliced off with pruning shears. Lana and Lilly had to edit out parts of their film that were not received well in order to better the film's chances at commercial success.

The finished product rose above many other similar movies released at the time. The neo-noir film about two women trying to survive in a male-dominated world showed off the Wachowskis' skill in stylized camerawork and

The Wachowskis worked with a feminist consultant to make the on-screen lesbian relationship between Jennifer Tilly and Gina Gershon's characters look natural.

technical filmmaking. A September 2012 retro-spective piece on the cult classic published on the A.V. Club called the film "a genuine bench-mark for LGBT cinema."

To avoid exploiting the two female charac-ters' relationship, the Wachowskis hired feminist Susie Bright to work as a sex consultant. Bright helped choreograph the romantic sequences in a realistic way, rather than one that could be seen as false or disingenuous. What results is a progressive love story that celebrates a realistic lesbian relationship—and not a Hollywood ver-sion of one. The LGBTQ community noticed the Wachowskis' work, and the film won an honor-able mention for the Grand Jury Award at the 1996 L.A. Outfest and a Gay and Lesbian Alli-ance against Defamation (GLAAD) Media Award for Outstanding Film in 1997.

Lana and Lilly's career changed after the movie was released. Lilly said, "After *Bound* we were offered a lot of lesbian thrillers." But much more than that had changed for Lana and Lilly. Aside from having a feature film on their résumé, they were now able to get into contact with powerful people in the film industry. Imme-diately following *Bound,* however, they had no idea how to follow up. Regarding the lack of clear direction, Lana later jokingly told the *New York*

Times, "Maybe we'll just retire with a two-film retrospective. We're just so tired at this point."

Of course, the Wachowskis did not retire. In fact, their biggest successes still lay ahead of them. Lilly and Lana continued to work well together. Neither of them recalls arguing much during their writing or directing processes. Their challenge was to continue their work, cultivate their industry relationships, and hope for a positive reception to their work. All of this would come together in a major way with their very next project, one that mixed genres in a way the Wachowski siblings had loved to do since their days in the attic playing Dungeons & Dragons with friends.

CHAPTER 3

ENTER THE MATRIX

Having just directed *Bound*, Lana Wachowski and her sister, Lilly, were on the cusp of major success. While Hollywood expected the directorial duo to create another lesbian thriller, they had something else in mind. Lana and Lilly had a script they had been working on for years, and they just needed a little help from their newfound bigwig connections to get it off the ground. That movie, *The Matrix*, would make them far more famous than they ever dreamed—or wanted.

CONSTRUCTING *THE MATRIX* (1999)

In 1994, Lana and Lilly completed the script for *The Matrix*. The film is set in a futuristic dystopia where machines have enslaved humanity while keeping humans comatose in pods. The people trapped in these pods are placated by having their minds in a continuous simulated reality called the Matrix. Only the film's hero and his friends are able to fight back against the machines and save humanity from its enslavement.

The idea for *The Matrix* came to Lana and Lilly while they were working on a comic book proposal. The concept of "worlds within worlds" interested the siblings, as did the use of virtual reality in movies. "And then it hit us," Lana later recalled in an interview with *The New Yorker,* "what if this world was the virtual world?" The story combined elements of philosophy with martial arts movies. The two received good feedback from various people. Their manager, Lawrence Mattis, said, "When I first read *The Matrix,* I called them all excited because they'd written a script about [French philosopher] Descartes."

Because of the success of their directorial debut *Bound,* Lana and Lilly were able to proceed with *The Matrix.* Still, the process was not easy. Everyone who received the script passed on it. Mattis recalls nobody "getting it." In the same *New Yorker* article, he shares, "To this day, I think Warner Bros. bought [*The Matrix*] half because of the relationship with them and half because they thought something was there." Lana and Lilly hired two of their friends who worked as cartoonists—including Steve Skroce, with whom they had worked at Marvel Comics—to create a comic book version of their script. It resulted in a six-hundred-page version of the movie that the Wachowskis showed to the studio. A producer noted that the comic book was identical to the movie. Their salesmanship worked. Between the impressive comic book and the success of *Bound*, Warner Brothers now had confidence in the Wachowskis.

The two directors credited the studio's president of worldwide production, Lorenzo di Bonaventura, for getting the movie approved. In an April 1999 article for the *New York Times*, Bonaventura commented, "When you read the script, you knew it was a new and different kind of movie. It had great action and great characters, and you got a sense of how important these filmmakers would become." Bonaventura was not scared off by the high concept of the film, and he felt that the Wachowskis would be able to pull off the visuals that people had a hard time understanding when reading the script. Lana and Lilly also credit movie producer Joel Silver for getting *The Matrix* into theaters. Lana joked

Lorenzo di Bonaventura is photographed at a June 30, 2014 press conference in Berlin, Germany.

that even though Silver produced the much-maligned *Assassins,* she and her brother forgave him and were willing to work with him again.

THE MAKING OF *THE MATRIX*

Turning their big, creative ideas into reality would not be an easy task. At the heart of *The Matrix* was the Wachowskis' longtime fascination with challenging our perception of reality. They would need to create two distinct worlds in order to achieve their concept of "worlds within worlds" while also incorporating mythological elements with the then-nascent Internet culture. At the time of the film's release, Lilly explained, "The script was a synthesis of ideas that sort of came together at a moment when we were interested in a lot of things: making mythology relevant in a modern context, relating quantum physics to Zen Buddhism, investigating your own life." It was obvious the Wachowskis were integrating many distinct ideas into one movie, as evidenced by their notebooks filled with ideas.

The fantastical nature of the screenplay required them to break new ground in terms of filmmaking and special effects. During this era of Hollywood, movies intended for broad audiences tended to be straightforward and easily digestible. Major studios were less willing to invest large amounts of money in something that could be seen as highbrow or esoteric. But Bonaventura tracked the script for four years and was responsible for pushing it through.

The movie took 118 days to shoot on a production budget of almost seventy million dollars. To save on budget, Warner Brothers decided to shoot the movie in Australia, a less expensive option than shooting in the United States, where production costs would have come closer to ninety-five million dollars. Taking into account the amount of special effects involved, however, *The Matrix* was a relatively cheap film to make compared to other films with the same special effects produced during that time.

The studio cast a mix of established movie stars, including Keanu Reeves and Laurence Fishburne, with new talent, and matched them with actors with whom they had previously worked, such as actor Joe Pantoliano. Actors Carrie-Anne Moss and Hugo Weaving rounded out the leading cast.

To create the right look and feel for their movie, Lana and Lilly studied work from various directors, including Hong Kong filmmakers such as John Woo and Hollywood directors George Lucas, John Huston, Billy Wilder, Ridley Scott, Fritz Lang, and their childhood idol Stanley Kubrick. They also reread a favorite book of theirs, *The Odyssey* by Homer. "I read it all the time," Lana said. "I always get something out of it."

Many film critics attributed the movie's success to the Wachowskis' mix of diverse, sometimes contrasting film genres. It differed from the standard action films that Warner Brothers had previously released by present-ing a blend of mythology, religious mysticism, martial arts, science fiction, and virtual reality.

Actor Keanu Reeves is photographed at the premiere of *The Matrix* on March 24, 1999.

It hit upon familiar tropes as well, with Keanu Reeves playing a computer hacker-turned-hero and Laurence Fishburne providing leadership and training to help achieve their ultimate goals. The lead actors all performed many of their own stunts and choreographed fights. Audiences saw these actors' weeks of martial arts training come to life on screen.

AN AWARD-WINNING BLOCKBUSTER

Lana and Lilly were not sure how their film would be received by the general public. They wanted to see if and how moviegoers would respond to an intellectual action film. "If audiences are sort of interested in movies that are made like McDonald's hamburgers, which do have a value in the world," Lana told the *New York Times* just prior to *The Matrix*'s release, "then we have to re-evaluate our entire career."

Lucky for Lana and Lilly, they did not have to reevaluate anything. Their once risky film idea had produced—and produced well—for Warner Brothers. Released March 31, 1999, *The Matrix* reached number one at the box office on its opening weekend, and the film grossed $37.2 million in its first five days. At the time, it was the largest Easter weekend opening in movie history according to Dan Fellman, the studio's

Poster for the film *The Matrix* (1999).

BULLET TIME

The Matrix uses myriad special effects and techniques to immerse the viewer in a world of killer machines, gravity-defying martial arts, and impossible acrobatics. However, inarguably the best-remembered effect from the film is something Lana and Lilly Wachowski dubbed bullet time. The seeds of the technique were actually planted in the 1870s by photographer Eadweard Muybridge, who famously set up a series of cameras to determine if a horse has all four legs off the ground while it gallops. (It does.)

"Bullet time" created the effect of a bullet traveling through space in slow motion using virtual cinematography to stitch together a series of shots. The signature effect was accomplished by first recording the actor against a green screen that would later be replaced with a digitally rendered background such as a rooftop. The visual effects team set up a rig of one hundred and twenty cameras that shot in rapid sequence around the actor, creating a series of still images of the action.

The effect would be imitated in various films after *The Matrix*. "Virtual cinematography" would become a buzzword, and bullet time would eventually become a trope itself. But when it debuted in *The Matrix*, it established the Wachowskis and their film as technically and stylistically innovative.

One of the most memorable special effects of *The Matrix* was bullet time.

president for distribution. Fellman credited the movie's success to the fact that it was "cutting-edge" and a unique offering in the cinema. "It just rocks," he put it succinctly. Eventually, *The Matrix* earned close to half a billion dollars worldwide and four Academy Awards.

The special effects for *The Matrix* were praised by many in the industry. The movie won the Academy Award for Best Visual Effects for the year, beating out the immensely popular *Star Wars: Episode 1—The Phantom Menace.* The CGI, or computer-generated imagery, movement in films began in earnest with the 1982 film *Tron* and reached a new high point with *The Matrix.* The Wachowskis played a big part in breaking new ground in special effects. The bar for visual effects production was raised, and the movie ushered in a new digital revolution in film. The era of optical, tactile effects was becoming outmoded as the Wachowskis went on to primarily use digital techniques in *The Matrix's* sequels.

EXPANDING *THE MATRIX*

With the massive success of *The Matrix*, it came as no surprise that two sequels were given the green-light for production. Lana and Lilly headed back to Australia to film both movies at the same time, with the plan to release them within months of each other. The sequels were titled *The Matrix Reloaded* and *The Matrix Revolutions.* They followed the further adventures of Neo, Trinity, and Laurence Fishburne's character, Morpheus, as they fight against machines for humanity's freedom.

The movies were released in May and November 2003, but they did not reach the success of the first film in the trilogy. Whereas the first film inspired numerous books and websites studying the blend of philosophy, kung fu, and cyberculture, the second and third movies were met with disappointment as audiences struggled to connect to the wider Matrix universe. Perhaps the notoriously troubled production came across in the films. Shooting the two movies took nearly three hundred days, and the enormous amount of work constructing a world from scratch took its toll on crewmembers.

Tragically, two actors died before filming their scenes. Furthermore, a crewmember committed suicide during production. Then the crewmember's girlfriend took a trip to Bali with her friend to recover, only to witness the friend's death in the 2002 Bali terrorist attack in which an Islamist terrorist group detonated bombs killing more than two hundred people.

Despite the tragedies that occurred during filming and lukewarm reception compared to the first movie in the series, the two sequels still earned more than a billion dollars globally.

The expansion of *The Matrix* brand wouldn't cease with sequel films. Lana and Lilly had been avid gamers their entire lives, so when they had the opportunity to expand *The Matrix* into the gaming world, they weren't going to let it pass. They initially tried to have a game produced in 1997, but they could not find a publisher. When the movie came out in 1999 and proved to be such a huge success, Lana and Lilly tried to convince Warner Brothers to create video games to accompany the sequels. The studio, however, was not interested.

In order to get their video game idea going, the Wachowskis made their own deal with game designer Shiny Entertainment and gave a share of the revenue to Warner Brothers. Rather than a direct adaptation of their movies, the game was a story that ran parallel to the main movie trilogy. The game, *Enter the Matrix*, came with a 244-page script and a twenty-one-million-dollar production budget.

The expansion of the film's brand, however, did put a strain on those working on it. The star of the games and costar of the movies,

Jada Pinkett Smith, had trouble understanding everything she was participating in. "I'm confused about what script is what," she told *Entertainment Weekly* in April 2003. "I had three of them, and they all intertwined: the video game, the sequel, and the third movie."

Lana and Lilly oversaw the game's development and shot extra footage for the game's designers to use. The game was released concurrently with the second Matrix movie, *The Matrix Reloaded*. Within a couple years, *Enter the Matrix* would go on to sell around six million copies worldwide. The game's success allowed them to create a follow-up called *The Matrix: Path of Neo* using footage from all three movies.

CHAPTER 4

OUT OF THE SPOTLIGHT

Prior to the release of *The Matrix*, many in the movie industry noted that the Wachowskis were down-to-earth and unaffected by the trappings of working in Hollywood. They were modest and reluctant to step into the public eye. After *The Matrix,* their attitude toward fame did not change, even in spite of the enormous success of their creation and pressure from the movie studio to promote their movies with interviews and public appearances. It was during this time that Lana came to terms with her self-image and hoped that her family would come to support her.

STAYING BEHIND THE SCENES

There were many things that Lana and Lilly

agreed on throughout their lives, chief among them their desire to stay anonymous. Lilly explained that she wanted to maintain her ability to walk into a comic book shop and not be recognized by any of her fans or fans of *The Matrix*. The siblings were not interested in becoming celebrities despite many opportunities to do so. "There's something nicely egalitarian about anonymity," Lilly would comment years later in 2012 to Aleksandar Hemon of *The New Yorker*.

In 2000, the Wachowskis made their last public appearance, including press and film premieres, for twelve years. The siblings have made it clear that their absence had nothing to do with gender or concern over how either would be received after transitioning. Lana described their world as contracting at an alarming rate after *The Matrix* was released in 1999. "We became acutely aware of the preciousness of anonymity," Lana explained in her 2012 HRC Visibility Award acceptance speech, "understanding it as a form of virginity, something you only lose once." Lana was unwilling to sacrifice her access to civic spaces, to live in the public without scrutiny, and an "egalitarian invisibility."

But the two kids from Chicago were pressed to do publicity to help promote their projects. Warner Brothers felt that it was essential that directors help sell and market a movie. Their stance on the matter was nonnegotiable. Yet Lana and Lilly were equally firm and refused to do any further press in the future. When pressed by the studio to choose between two options—either make movies or not do press—the Wachowskis were clear in their choice; they told Warner Brothers that they would prefer not to make movies. According to Lana, Warner Brothers changed its position and said, "Hang on. Maybe there's a little room for negotiation."

Lana and Lilly signed a contract with Warner Brothers, one that included a no-press clause. The industry press and the accompanying media glare were no longer concerns for the two, and they gave no interviews and did no publicity. Along with avoiding any press requirements, their contract also stated that they would not be photographed or quoted in the promotional material used for *The Matrix Reloaded* and *The Matrix Revolutions*. Rather than live in Hollywood as celebrities, Lana and Lilly opted to stay close to home in Chicago, where they could be near their family.

"They love everything about moviemaking except one thing: the press," producer Joel Silver shared in a May 2003 *USA TODAY* article aptly titled "Brothers Eschew *Matrix* Hype."

Poster for the film *The Matrix Reloaded* (2003).

"They want their films to do the talking for them." Filming the *Matrix* sequels in Australia helped them avoid the Los Angeles press junket associated with the films. Their aversion to press even extended to the crew on their movie sets. Crewmembers on the set of *The Matrix Reloaded* were reportedly instructed to avoid talking with the directors and to keep at least twenty feet away. Carrie-Anne Moss, the actress who portrays Trinity in the films said, "They don't talk a lot, but they will shoot a scene over and over until everything is exactly right."

During the shooting of both sequels to *The Matrix*, the Wachowskis kept very private lives. Shown here is a scene from *The Matrix Reloaded* (2003).

DIVORCE FROM BLOOM

While Lana Wachowski was in Australia shooting the final two movies in the *Matrix* trilogy, she was going through troubles in her personal life. Her marriage to Thea Bloom was dissolving. In December 2002, Bloom filed for divorce. A legal battle between Wachowski and her estranged wife ensued. The court papers reveal more details of Wachowski's life outside of her work.

During divorce proceedings, Bloom stated that Wachowski "[had] been extremely dishonest with me in our personal life." Bloom goes

on to claim that the couple's separation was "based on very intimate circumstances concerning which I do not elaborate at this time for the reasons of his personal privacy." Rumors began swirling about Wachowski's personal life, and many outlets reported that Wachowski was a transvestite—a person who dresses in a way typically associated with a gender other than the one with which they personally identify.

To further complicate matters, Bloom filed a breach-of-contract suit regarding an alleged prenuptial agreement signed before her wedding to Wachowski in 1993. The suit claimed that that Lana and Lilly Wachowski began to create *The Matrix* franchise after Bloom and Lana Wachowski were already married, something which, if true, would entitle Bloom to a share of the millions of dollars in earnings resulting from the successful series. The Wachowskis declined to comment publicly on the situation, but in court defended the idea that *The Matrix* predated Lana's marriage to Bloom.

COMING OUT AS TRANSGENDER

It was during this same period in her life that Wachowski decided to come out to her family. Wachowski was with her sister, Lilly, in Australia filming *The Matrix* sequels. In addition to her divorce, Wachowski's gender dysphoria was causing her to suffer from depression. She would later admit that she had trouble even saying the words "transgender" or "transsexual." She would eventually find the strength to say those words and tell others about her gender identity.

As she became more confident about outwardly expressing her gender, Wachowski wanted to tell her parents and siblings. The thought of doing so made her incredibly uneasy. She suffered from insomnia and would not sleep for days on end. Luckily, she had help from a therapist, who helped develop a long-term plan for coming out. "It was going to take three years. Maybe five," Lana explained. "A couple of weeks into the plan, my mom called." From abroad, Lynne Wachowski called her daughter, and sensing something was bothering her child, she immediately flew to Australia with her husband.

Lynne was distraught on the plane, afraid that she would lose her child. She confessed to Lana that she was fearful to arrive and discover that Lana had committed suicide. However, the experience was not one of loss, but one of discovery. When Lynne arrived, Lana told her mother the truth: "I'm transgender. I'm a girl."

Wachowski would recall the conversation with her mother during her 2012 HRC Visibility Award acceptance speech as a "big, tear-soaked baptism." Lynne's fear of loss was quickly replaced by a feeling of discovery. Instead of losing a child, Lynne learned that there was more to her child than she had known before. The discovery of a new side to Lana, a part that was previously unseen to her, was taken as a gift by Lynne.

Wachowski's father, Ron, was also unconditional in his support. As were her sisters.
According to Wachowski, her father shrugged
off her announcement with no trouble. He told
her, "Look, if my kid wants to sit down and talk
to me, I'm a lucky man. What matters is that
you're alive, you seem happy, and that I can
put my arms around you and give you a kiss."

Lilly, who had worked so closely with Lana
for years, already had suspicions about Lana's
gender identity for some time before Lana came
out. Their relationship improved thereafter,
and later, Lilly would also come out as a trans
woman. Before transitioning, Lana took out her
frustrations on other people, including Lilly. After
transition, Lana became "much more open-
minded. She's a lot easier to work with than Larry
[Lana Wachowski's name prior to transitioning]."
According to Ron Wachowski, his daughters
"have the best marriage I have ever seen."

A few days after coming out to her family, Lana and the rest of the Wachowski family
went out to dinner in Sydney. Lana's outfit was
feminine, one of her first public expressions of
her gender identity. Wachowski hoped strang-
ers would see her as a woman. She hoped that,
"Waiters would not call me 'sir' or 'he,'" Lana
later explained, "as if these people suddenly

had the power to confirm or deny my existence." Lynne introduced Lana as her daughter to the waitress, who replied, "Wow, she looks just like you." Lana returned to filming the next day outwardly expressing her gender identity as if nothing had happened.

MEDIA SCRUTINY

Meanwhile, the Wachowskis' movies were making millions at the box office—*The Matrix Reloaded* made $93.3 million in its opening weekend—and the siblings were becoming extremely wealthy. They owned homes in Venice Beach, California, but preferred to stay closer to their hometown of Chicago. Even in Chicago, several neighbors noted that the Wachowskis kept to themselves. Despite their best efforts to stay away from the media, the Wachowskis were not able to completely extricate themselves from public life.

After Lana Wachowski came out to her family, numerous reports began to spread about her gender identity. News outlets were interested in the veracity of the rumors. Lynne and Ron Wachowski became the targets of reporters and the media as they camped out in front of the Wachowski home in Chicago, occasionally ringing their doorbell attempting to get the scoop.

NATIONAL CENTER FOR TRANSGENDER EQUALITY

Transgender equality is one of the more recent civil rights movements to gain prominent national attention in the history of the United States. In 2003, the National Center for Transgender Equality (NCTE) was founded in Washington, DC. The original staff was small, but they all saw a need for policy changes to protect the transgender community in the United States and to assert transgender equality in laws. Their mission statement makes clear that they are a national social justice organization focused on ending discrimination and violence against the transgender community.

Their projects include the Racial and Economic Justice Initiative (REJI). In 2015, REJI's work aimed to improve conditions for transgender people in correctional facilities and those in immigration detention. The broader goal is to protect and include transgender people of color in both rural and urban poverty regions. Their initiatives work in conjunction with other racial, social, economic, and criminal justice movements on federal, state, and local levels.

Another of the NCTE's projects, the Trans Legal Services Network (TLSN), helps transgender individuals in legal matters including legal name changes and reporting their correct gender to the government, as well as other legal hurdles members of the transgender community may face. Since its inception, the NTCE has expanded nationwide. By early 2016, the NCTE was made up of over fifty organizations that service the transgender community.

On January 10, 2015, transgender rights activists marched in response to the suicide of a transgender teenager from Ohio on a month prior.

Lilly and Lana's long-held desire to stay out of the spotlight was incorrectly perceived to be merely a symptom of Lana's transition. Lilly would report the same experience years later after she, too, had privately transitioned from male to female, but had not yet publicly announced her gender identity. She came out as transgender in March 2016—only after reporters aggressively pursued her and threatened to publish stories about her gender identity.

As Lana experienced media scrutiny, the Wachowski family—especially Lilly—protected her. Years after coming out publicly, a reporter veered away from asking about their films to inquiring about Lana's gender. Lilly was quick to intervene. "Look, just so we're clear, if somebody asks something or says something about my sister that I don't like, understand that I will break a bottle over their head." While violence is not condonable, Lilly's defense of her sister is admirable. Lana Wachowski knew that she had her family's full support. When Lilly was ready to come out, she would also feel unconditional love and support from her family.

CHAPTER 5

FILM WORK AFTER
THE MATRIX

Lana Wachowski had successfully come out to her family and friends, and *The Matrix* sequels were completed. She and Lilly followed up *The Matrix* trilogy with new projects unrelated to the franchise.

Wachowski now had a freedom in her personal and professional life. "My biggest fears were all about losing my family," Lana explained. "Once they accepted me, everything else has been a piece of cake."

V FOR VENDETTA (2006)

The next project for Lana and her sister, Lilly, was *V for Vendetta*. Rather than direct the film themselves, the Wachowskis wrote the screenplay, and James McTeigue took over the director's

Director James McTeigue stands on the red carpet at a film premiere on April 23, 2013.

chair. The movie is based on a graphic novel of the same name, cocreated by Alan Moore and David Lloyd. Originally released in a monthly magazine in 1981, the full story was finally published in 1989 by DC Comics. The political thriller is set in the near future and is the story of a woman who gets caught up in a man's war against an oppressive government.

Lana and Lilly had a difficult time adapting a screenplay from the original work. Alan Moore was very publicly against the idea of a movie based on his work and made his displeasure known in the media. Lana said that without David Lloyd's support, they would have thrown out the entire project. However, Lloyd liked the Wachowskis' take on the graphic novel and felt that it was a good representation. "It always felt like an idea that could be transposed to other forms of media," Lloyd said. "In any of my work, the only expectation and desire is that the spirit and key elements are retained and the same essential message is captured."

V for Vendetta starred Hugo Weaving as the masked vigilante V, Natalie Portman as the protagonist Evey, and John Hurt as the head of the evil government Chancellor Sutler. Joel Silver, the same producer from *The Matrix*, also produced this film. The movie did solid business at the box office, and it came in first in its opening weekend at a little over $25 million dollars. On a budget of $54 million dollars, it went on to gross $132 million worldwide. The reviews were generally positive, and the film was a success for the Wachowskis.

One lasting image from the movie is the main character's Guy Fawkes mask. Fawkes was a sixteenth-century Englishman who plotted to blow up the English Parliament during a visit by King James I on November 5, 1605. He was caught before carrying out his plan and was

V for Vendetta helped re-popularize the infamous Guy Fawkes mask, as seen in here in a still from the film.

eventually executed along with other members of his group. The mask from the movie has been used by various activist groups, notably the hacking collective Anonymous, as a symbol of political dissent and protest.

SPEED RACER (2008)

Lana and Lilly's first directorial effort after *The Matrix* trilogy was a big-screen adaptation of the Japanese cartoon series *Speed Racer.* Their long-time collaborator Joel Silver took on the role of producer yet again, and the film was released by Warner Brothers. The Japanese cartoon series was about a race car driver named Speed, his top-of-the-line car the Mach 5, and the adventures he got into with his family.

By the time the Wachowskis came onboard for the project in 2006, Silver had already been working on a film adaptation of *Speed Racer* for over a decade. Silver worked with the Wachowskis for months to work out various elements of the movie adaptation. Their plan was to reach a wide audience. "I've struggled with this movie for a long time, but when [Lana] and Lilly came across with their ideas and vision, it was so fresh and original that you'd wonder why nobody else thought of it," Silver told *Deadline Hollywood* in October 2006.

Silver's production team had been happy with the experience of shooting in Europe for *V for Vendetta*, and they looked forward to returning for *Speed Racer* in the summer of 2007. The film starred Emile Hirsch as the eponymous Speed, Christina Ricci as his girlfriend, Trixie, and Matthew Fox as the mysterious Racer X. In addition to directing, Lana and her sister wrote the screenplay. They brought back many of their award-winning collaborators from *The Matrix.*

In 2008, the Wachowskis returned to the director's chair for *Speed Racer*, an adaptation of the Japanese cartoon series of the same name.

Although the successful **Matrix** team had been reassembled, **Speed Racer** did not fare as well at the box office. When it was released in the summer of 2008, it placed a disappointing third place for the weekend with an opening weekend total of $18.6 million. However, the average audience grade of the film was a healthy A− among a wide demographic.

Years after its underwhelming initial release, the film has found success as new audiences

discover it. A small cult following of fans who praise the film has developed online. Many appreciate the risks the Wachowskis took with the film's overall look and the bright colors they used.

CLOUD ATLAS (2012)

The next directorial effort by Lana and Lilly was a

WOMEN DIRECTORS BY THE NUMBERS

In 2012, the Sundance Institute and Women in Film Los Angeles created the Female Filmmakers Initiative with the goal of increasing the number of women working on the production side of films. They studied the numbers behind the films at the Sundance Film Festival (SFF) from 2002 through 2012 to determine the obstacles and opportunities women face in the U.S. independent film industry.

The initiative's study found that women directed about 25 percent of the films in the SFF's U.S. Dramatic Competition each year between 2002 and 2014. That's a three-to-one men-to-women gender ratio for directors. The study also found that films with male directors were more likely to receive distribution from companies with greater resources and reach than films with female directors. Those companies distributing movies directed by women had fewer financial resources or industry clout.

When the field of study was limited to big-budget movies backed by large studios, the gender gap was even wider. For films shown on more than 250 screens, male directors outnumbered female directors six to one. Of the 1,300 top-grossing films from 2002 to 2014, about 4 percent of the films were directed by women, a twenty-three-to-one men-to-women ratio.

In the years since its inception, the Female Filmmakers Initiative has worked to provide greater awareness, financing, artist support, and networking opportunities for its women filmmakers. It continues to work to fight gender inequality in Hollywood. In October 2015, it organized a summit of forty top Hollywood decision makers to discuss potential systemic changes that might level out the playing field.

film adaptation of the best-selling 2004 novel *Cloud Atlas*, written by David Mitchell. They codirected the 2012 film with German director Tom Tykwer. The idea for the movie came about in 2005 during the filming of *V for Vendetta*. Lana Wachowski noticed Natalie Portman reading *Cloud Atlas* on set. Portman was enthusiastic about the book. Wachowski soon read it herself and shared it with Lilly. They were both hooked.

The movie is a complicated weave of six story lines. The difficult-to-produce screenplay was written by the Wachowskis and Tykwer together. The distinct stories are interlocking and entail a large cast of characters spanning multiple locations and centuries. The book was so complex that its author, David Mitchell, doubted that it could ever be turned into a film. But the Wachowskis were determined to do just that as they worked with Tykwer in a rented house in Costa Rica. Their breakthrough idea was to have the same actors play multiple characters in the different stories so that the film would be more cohesive and retain a central theme. Their model for *Cloud Atlas* was *2001: A Space Odyssey*, the film that had made such a lasting impression during Lana's youth. Starring in the film were Tom Hanks, Halle Berry, and Jim Sturgess, among others.

The movie was a difficult one to sell to a wide audience, a fact that many of those involved with the production were aware of before the movie was released. The film's star, Tom Hanks, said, "The script was not user-friendly. The demands it put upon the audience and everybody, the business risk, were off the scale."

In the end, the film did not perform well at the U.S. box office. In its opening weekend, *Cloud Atlas* came in third place with a gross of $9.4 million. Reviews were mixed, and it had the unfortunate timing of opening the same weekend that Hurricane Sandy hit the Northeast United States. Fortunately, it did perform well internationally, where intellectual movies are a

Actors Halle Berry and Tom Hanks co-starred in *Cloud Atlas* (2012).

bigger draw than in the United States. *Cloud Atlas* performed particularly well in China, where the movie was cut by twenty-three minutes to appease the country's censors.

JUPITER ASCENDING (2015)

For their next project, Lana and Lilly direced an original screenplay called *Jupiter Ascending.* Lana Wachowski described the movie as a science fiction space opera at an Australians in Film Awards & Benefit Gala Dinner.

Writing and filming the project was a less complicated undertaking than *Cloud Atlas's* multi-layered story line. Even still, Wachowski admitted that keeping things small did not come naturally. "We seem not to be very good at making small things. We keep saying 'Let's go make a small movie.' But then they always end up being enormously complex." The Wachowskis preferred to try something new and different in cinema.

They cast Channing Tatum and Mila Kunis as the leads, with Sean Bean and Eddie Redmayne as supporting cast members. Kunis stars as a woman who learns that she is a galactic princess. Tatum plays an alien who comes to help her in her quest as they avoid the villain played by Redmayne. The film featured romance and complicated visual effects to complement the action. Lana and Lilly oversaw the special effects and editing.

Despite the poor box office performances of their previous two films, the Wachowskis were hopeful that they would be able to connect with audiences even if the financial goals were not met. "People come up to us and just break into tears talking about [*Cloud Atlas*]," Lana said in an October 2013 interview with the Associated Press. She went on

Mila Kunis and Channing Tatum stand on the red carpet at the Los Angeles premiere of *Jupiter Ascending* on February 2, 2015.

to mention that many fans call *Speed Racer* their favorite movie.

Jupiter Ascending was released on February 6, 2015. Although its box office numbers were disappointing in the United States, the movie did well in internationally. It opened earning a strong $23.2 million in China, making it the number one movie in the country its first weekend. It made well over $100 million in foreign markets.

CHAPTER 6

BECOMING VISIBLE

For a director who so valued her privacy and anonymity, speaking to the press about her gender identity and stepping out for the whole world to see was an unlikely move. But after years working in Hollywood and with a number of filmmaking accolades under her belt, Wachowski took this brave step and showed the world who she truly was.

"HI, I'M LANA"

After her 2002 divorce from Thea Bloom, Wachowski eventually met and fell in love with another woman named Karin Winslow. In 2009, they were married. True to character, Lana Wachowski keeps her marriage private and has never publicly discussed it. (It should be noted that sexual orientation—the sex to which an individual is attracted—and gender identity are unrelated. After transitioning, Lana Wachowski still dates and is sexually attracted to women.)

One thing Wachowski decided was worth making public, however, was her gender identity. She was well aware of the questions she would face and the debates she might inspire. Understandably, she had hesitations. Wachowski had to overcome feelings of being an outsider, broken, or unlovable. She was horrified by the interrogation and confession format of talk shows and confessional interviews. She was also concerned that, although she might receive blanket acceptance from LGBTQ organizations, coming out might not change anything for the greater transgender population.

Because of her and her sister's intensely private nature, Lana's coming out would be the first time she spoke publicly after her transition. She made the decision to come out as trans while she and her sister were making *Cloud Atlas.* In that film, a particular character with whom Lana related had the line, "If I had remained invisible, the truth would have remained hidden and I couldn't allow that." One of the themes of the movie, people's responsibilities to one another, spurred her on. A few months before *Cloud*

During the shooting of *Cloud Atlas*, Lana Wachowski decided to come out as transgender. Here she stands before media at the Los Angeles premiere of the movie on October 24, 2012.

Atlas hit theaters, Wachowski, her sister (who had not yet transitioned from male to female), and codirector Tom Tykwer released a short two-and-a-half-minute video introducing the movie. Making no special mention of her transition, Wachowski simply introduced herself as Lana to the camera—and the world.

The announcement was met with a muted response. Perhaps this was because of Lana's general anonymity; the public hardly knew her prior to her transition. Others suggest that the collective shrug was a result of the fact that the "secret" was already in tabloids for years following Wachowski's divorce. Wachowski had gradually shared her transition with friends over the years. Most people close to her were already well aware of her gender identity. Coming out to the general public was the final brave step in being open about her identity. Many in the entertainment industry applauded Wachowski's courage and offered their full support.

AWARDS AND RECOGNITION

Wachowski received a great deal of support after coming out. Her high-profile career and ability to communicate ideas made her an ideal candidate to become an advocate for the transgender movement. She was asked to speak at numerous events and accept a variety of awards.

THE HUMAN RIGHTS CAMPAIGN'S VISIBILITY AWARD

The Human Rights Campaign (HRC) had asked Lana Wachowski to appear at HRC events multiple times, but she always declined because of issues with scheduling. They contacted her again after she posted her coming-out video in 2012, and Wachowski happened to have plans to be in San Francisco, the location of the event, at the same time in October. She took the coincidence as a sign that it was time to finally agree.

The HRC gave Lana the Visibility Award for publicly acknowledging her gender identity despite her aversion to being in the press and media. Chad Griffin, president of the HRC, said, "Lana's willingness to tell her story will impact and change countless lives across the world." He believed that Lana's success in Hollywood would help inspire others in the LGBTQ community to reach for such lofty goals.

Wachowski was willing to sacrifice the privacy she had defended for so long to help others. In her speech she said, "I hope to offer their

The formerly camera-shy Wachowski speaks at a press conference for *Cloud Atlas* during the Toronto International Film Festival on September 9, 2012.

love in the form of my materiality to a project like this one started by the HRC, so that this world that we imagine in this room might be used to gain access to other rooms, to other worlds previously unimaginable." The response to Lana's speech was overwhelmingly positive. Many in attendance told Wachowski how affected they were by her speech.

2014 EQUALITY ILLINOIS FREEDOM AWARD

On February 8, 2014, Equality Illinois presented Wachowski with the 2014 Equality Freedom Award. The organization is the oldest and largest in Illinois that fights for LGBTQ rights in the state. They wanted to recognize Wachowski's brave decision to sacrifice her privacy to inspire others in the transgender community. According to Equality Illinois, the award is given every year to people who display a certain level of "vision, courage, and leadership in the effort to achieve full equality for LGBT individuals in Illinois."

Equality Illinois' CEO, Bernard Cherkasov, said in a statement that Lana's choice "to share her story with a world that needs to hear her account of growing up transgendered [*sic*] is worthy of recognition with the Equality Illinois Freedom Award." Wachowski was humbled by

TRANS IN THE WHITE HOUSE: RAFFI FREEDMAN-GURSPAN

In 2015, the Obama administration announced the first openly transgender official appointed to serve in the White House. Raffi Freedman-Gurspan was hired as the outreach and recruitment director for presidential personnel in the White House Office of Presidential Personnel. Prior to the new appointment, Freedman-Gurspan was a policy advisor for the National Center for Transgender Equality's Racial and Economic Justice Initiative. The White House recruitment director is responsible for directing presidential personnel staffers who recruit candidates to serve the president in various departments and agencies while also meeting the personnel priorities of the administration.

There had previously been transgender people appointed to presidential commissions and boards, but Freedman-Gurspan was the first openly trans appointee to work at the White House. Senior Adviser Valerie Jarrett said in a statement that Freedman-Gurspan's "commitment to bettering the lives of transgender Americans, particularly transgender people of color and those in poverty, reflects the values of this Administration."

Freedman-Gurspan has a history of helping others, including those in the transgender community. Among other initiatives, she fought to improve prison conditions for transgender inmates and developed solutions to address violence against transgender women of color. She was the first openly transgender woman working at the Massachusetts State House, as well. Freedman-Gurspan's appointment has been hailed as a major victory by LGBTQ advocates and certainly breaks new ground in the continuing diversification of the United States.

the award and the organization's work in her home state.

TRANS 100 KEYNOTE

Every year in Chicago, an event called the Trans 100 takes place to celebrate the top activists in the trans community. In 2015, Lana Wachowski was asked to serve as the keynote speaker. It gave her a chance to share things with a trans audience that she would not have shared with a broader, general audience. She spoke about the dangers the transgender community faces for simply expressing who they are inside, but also the strength they have to keep on fighting for equality. "First, our dream to be seen and accepted as trans people can often cost us our lives," Lana said.

"And second, none of us in here has ever given up on that dream."

FOR THE WORLD TO SEE

What would have been unthinkable decades ago has happened in recent years as more and more transgender actors and characters appear in television shows and movies. One of the best received of these shows has been *Transparent*, a show about a seventy-year-old father in a Jewish family who comes out as a transgender woman and the impact it has on her three children. The show's first season won five Emmy Awards, including Outstanding Lead Actor in a Comedy Series and a directing award for director and show creator Jill Soloway.

Soloway created the show based on similar experiences in her own family. She sees *Transparent* as more than a television show. In a September 2015 interview with the *Washington Post* she said, "We are part of a civil rights movement. We didn't really set out to necessarily be part of a movement, but that's how we found ourselves."

In 2015, the Wachowskis released season one of a new web television series, *Sense8*. The show

In 2015, the Wachowskis released the first season of their web television series *Sense8*, starring transgender actor Jamie Clayton (shown in the above still from the series) as a political blogger and activist.

features a transgender character played by transgender actor Jamie Clayton. Clayton's character is a political blogger and activist in San Francisco. Notably, Clayton's character's storyline does not focus on her gender identity, but rather her life, relationship, and friends. Clayton describes working with Wachowski as a unique experience. "It's so authentic and human," Clayton said in an August 2015 interview with GLAAD. She says, "[her character] is a survivor and a hero. Just like Lana."

The most direct impact of Lana's bravery and authenticity was on her own sister, Lilly. In March 2016, Lilly came out as transgender. After facing threats that *The Daily Mail* would report her gender identity, Lilly chose to beat them to the punch.

On March 8, 2016, Lilly Wachowski released a statement to the *Windy City Times*. She stated, "I knew at some point I would have to come out publicly…I just wanted—needed some time to get my head right, to feel comfortable." Wachowski rightly criticized the press for forcing her to come out sooner than she would have preferred. She also credited Lana with having blazed a trail. Lilly joined her sister as a pioneer for trans rights.

Over time, the shy and reclusive Lana Wachowski was able to admit to herself that being transgender did not make her unlovable and isolated. She learned that she had a greater purpose to be visible and help others—such as her sister. Lana Wachowski bravely stepped forward for the world to see her as she is. At the HRC award ceremony, she shared her thoughts: "Invisibility is indivisible from visibility; for the transgender this is not simply a philosophical conundrum—it can be the difference between life and death."

TIMELINE

June 21, 1965 Lana Wachowski is born in Chicago, Illinois, to Ron and Lynne Wachowski.

December 29, 1967 Lana's sister and professional partner, Lilly Wachowski, is born.

1993 The Wachowskis begin writing for Marvel Comics' *Ectokid* series.

October 30, 1993 Lana Wachowski marries a woman named Thea Bloom.

October 4, 1996 *Bound*, cowritten and codirected by Lana and Lilly Wachowski, is released.

1996 *Bound* receives an honorable mention for the Grand Jury Award at the L.A. Outfest.

1997 *Bound* receives a GLAAD Media Award for Outstanding Film.

March 31, 1999 *The Matrix* is released and becomes a box-office success.

December 2002 Wachowski and her wife, Thea Bloom, file for divorce.

May 14, 2003 *Enter the Matrix*, a video game that takes place within the same universe as *The Matrix* and its sequels, is released. The video game is written and directed by the Wachowskis.

May 15, 2003 The first sequel to *The Matrix*, *The Matrix Reloaded*, is released.

November 5, 2003 The third movie in the

Matrix trilogy, *The Matrix Revolutions*, is released.

March 22, 2005 *The Matrix Online*, a multi-player online game written and directed by the Wachowskis, is released.

November 8, 2005 *The Matrix: Path of Neo*, another video game written and directed by the Wachowskis, is released.

March 17, 2006 *V for Vendetta* is released.

May 9, 2008 The Wachowskis' movie adaptation of the Japanese animated series *Speed Racer* is released.

2009 Lana Wachowski marries her second wife, Karin Winslow.

November 25, 2009 The Wachowski-produced film *Ninja Assassin* is released.

July 26, 2012 Lana Wachowski makes her first public appearance after transitioning in an online promotional video for *Cloud Atlas*.

October 20, 2012 Lana receives the Visibility Award at the Human Rights Campaign's annual San Francisco gala dinner.

October 26, 2012 *Cloud Atlas*, a movie codirected by the Wachowskis and Tom Tykwer and based on a 2004 novel of the same name, is released.

February 8, 2014 Lana receives the 2014 Equality Illinois Freedom Award.

February 6, 2015 *Jupiter Ascending* is released.

June 5, 2015 *Sense8*, a web TV series released on Netflix and cocreated by the Wachowskis, stars a transgender character played by a transgender actor.

March 8, 2016 Lana Wachowski's sister, Lilly, comes out publicly as transgender and announces her transition from male to female.

GLOSSARY

B MOVIE A low-budget movie, especially (formerly) one made for use as a companion to the main attraction in a double feature.

CISGENDER A person whose gender identity is consistent with the gender they were assigned at birth.

CISNORMATIVITY The common perception or use of language that assumes that all people are inherently cisgender and that transgender individuals are a deviation from a perceived norm.

CONUNDRUM A confusing and difficult problem or question.

CREDENTIALS Qualities, skills, or experience that make a person qualified to carry out a certain task or job.

DISSENT To differ in opinion.

DYSTOPIA An imagined place or state in which everything is unpleasant or bad, typically a totalitarian or environmentally degraded one.

EPONYMOUS Of or relating to the person or thing after which something is named.

ESOTERIC Hard to understand or of special or unusual interest.

GENDER IDENTITY A person's internal sense of gender often expressed through behavior, clothing, hairstyle, voice, or body characteristics.

INTOLERANT Unwilling to allow certain groups of people to have equality, freedom, or other social rights.

LGBTQ An acronym for "Lesbian, Gay, Bisexual, Transgender, and Queer/Questioning." Also commonly given as LGBT.

MONOLITH A single great stone, often in the form of a monument or column.

NASCENT Recently coming into existence.

OPTION To acquire the exclusive right to use a work as a basis for a film.

PRECONCEPTION An opinion or idea formed about somebody or something before any direct experience with the person or thing.

PREJUDICE A discriminatory dislike of a group of people based on race, sex, gender, religion, or other categorization of people.

STYLIZED Designed or represented according to an artistic style rather than according to nature or convention.

TRANSGENDER A person whose gender identity is inconsistent with the gender they were assigned at birth.

TRANSSEXUAL An older term used in the medical community to designate transgender individuals who seek surgical intervention so that their body's anatomy corresponds to their gender identity.

FOR MORE INFORMATION

COLAGE
3815 South Othello Street, Suite 100, #310
Seattle, WA 98118
(855) 4-COLAGE
Website: http://www.colage.org
COLAGE brings together people with LGBTQ
   parents to support them as they become
   leaders in the LGBTQ and ally communities.

Gay & Lesbian Alliance Against Defamation
   (GLAAD)
104 West 29th Street, 4th Floor
New York, NY 10001
(212) 629-3322
Website: http://www.glaad.org
GLAAD promotes positive representations of
   LGBTQ individuals in the media, working
   to ensure that the rights and dignity of the
   LGBTQ community are respected.

Gender Proud
E-mail: hello@genderproud.com
Website: http://www.genderproud.com
Founded by trans woman model Geena
   Rocero, Gender Proud's advocacy work is
   directed at expanding gender marker rights,
   helping transgender people change their

legal documentation to match their chosen name and gender identity.

National Center for Transgender Equality (NCTE)
1400 16th Street NW, Suite 510
Washington, DC 20036
(202) 642-4542
Website: http://www.transequality.org
Founded in 2003, the NCTE is a national social justice organization that advocates for policy reform to end discrimination and violence against transgender people and promote awareness of national issues of importance to transgender rights.

Transgender Law Center
1629 Telegraph Avenue, Suite 400
Oakland, CA 94612
(415) 865-0176
Website: http://transgenderlawcenter.org
The Transgender Law Center is dedicated to changing laws and policy so that members of the transgender community can live free from discrimination.

Trans People of Color Coalition (TPOCC)
E-mail: info@tpocc.org

Website: http://www.transpoc.org
The TPOCC is a national social justice organization working to advocate for the special
interests and rights of trans people of color.

TransYouth Family Allies (TYFA)
P.O. Box 1471
Holland, MI 49422
(888) 462-8932
Website: http://www.imatyfa.org
TYFA works to empower trans youth and their
families to create safe, understanding envi-
ronments in which they can grow up.

WEBSITES

Because of the changing nature of Internet
links, Rosen Publishing has developed an
online list of websites related to the subject of
this book. This site is updated regularly. Please
use this link to access this list:

http://www.rosenlinks.com/TGP/lana

FOR FURTHER READING

Andrews, Arin. *Some Assembly Required: The Not-So-Secret Life of a Transgender Teen.* New York, NY: Simon & Schuster, 2014.

Beemyn, Genny, and Sue Rankin. *The Lives of Transgender People.* New York, NY: Columbia University Press, 2011.

Chiang, Howard. *Transgender China.* New York, NY: Palgrave Macmillan, 2012.

Dohrenwend, Anne. *Coming Around: Parenting Lesbian, Gay, Bisexual, and Transgender Kids.* Far Hills, NJ: New Horizon Press, 2012.

Dzmura, Noach. *Balancing on the Mechitza: Transgender in Jewish Community.* Berkeley, CA: North Atlantic Books, 2010.

Enke, Anne. *Transfeminist Perspectives in and beyond Transgender and Gender Studies.* Philadelphia, PA: Temple University Press, 2012.

Espejo, Roman. *Transgender People.* Farmington Hills, MI: Greenhaven Press, 2011.

Hines, Sally. *Transgender Identities: Towards a Social Analysis of Gender Diversity.* New York, NY: Routledge, 2010.

Howell, Ally Windsor. *Transgender Persons and the Law.* Chicago, IL: American Bar Association, 2013.

Huegel, Kelly. *GLBTQ: The Survival Guide for Gay, Lesbian, Bisexual, Transgender, and*

Questioning Teens. 2nd ed. Minneapolis, MN: Free Spirit Publishing, 2011.

Kugle, Scott Alan. *Homosexuality in Islam: Critical Reflection on Gay, Lesbian, and Transgender Muslims.* Oxford, UK: Oneworld, 2010.

Kuklin, Susan. *Beyond Magenta: Transgender Teens Speak Out.* Somerville, MA: Candlewick Press, 2014.

Mills, Kirstin. *Transgender Lives: Complex Stories, Complex Voices.* Minneapolis, MN: Twenty-First Century Books, 2015.

Nadal, Kevin L. *That's So Gay! Microaggressions and the Lesbian, Gay, Bisexual, and Transgender Community.* Washington, DC: American Psychological Association, 2013.

Pepper, Rachel. *Transitions of the Heart: Stories of Love, Struggle and Acceptance by Mothers of Transgender and Gender Variant Children.* Berkeley, CA: Cleis Press, 2012.

Rupp, Leila J. *Understanding and Teaching U.S. Lesbian, Gay, Bisexual, and Transgender History.* Madison, WI: University of Wisconsin Press, 2014.

Schilt, Kristen. *Just One of the Guys? Transgender Men and the Persistence of Gender Inequality.* Chicago, IL: University of Chicago Press, 2010.

Schroth, Laura. *Trans Bodies, Trans Selves: A Resource for the Transgender Community.* New York, NY: Oxford University Press, 2014.

Shultz, Jackson Wright. *Trans/portraits: Voices from Transgender Communities.* Hanover, NH: Dartmouth College Press, 2015.

Teich, Nicholas M., and Jamison Green. *Transgender 101: A Simple Guide to a Complex Issue.* New York, NY: Columbia University Press, 2012.

Witten, Tarynn. *Gay, Lesbian, Bisexual, & Transgender Aging: Challenges in Research, Practice, and Policy.* Baltimore, MD: Johns Hopkins University Press, 2012.

BIBLIOGRAPHY

Abramovitch, Seth. "*Cloud Atlas* Director Lana Wachowski on Coming-Out Speech." *The Hollywood Reporter*. October 24, 2012. Retrieved November 24, 2015 (http://www. hollywoodreporter.com/news/cloud-atlas -director-lana-wachowski-382144).

Abramovitch, Seth. "Lana Wachowski Reveals Suicide Plan, Painful Past in Emotional Speech (Exclusive Video)." *The Hollywood Reporter*. October 24, 2012. Retrieved November 24, 2015 (http://www .hollywoodreporter.com/news/lana -wachowski-reveals-suicide-plan-382169).

American Psychological Association. "Answers to Your Questions about Transgender People, Gender Identity and Gender Expression." Retrieved October 19, 2015 (http:// www.apa.org/topics/lgbt/transgender.aspx).

Baim, Tracy. "Second Wachowski Filmmaker Sibling Comes Out as Trans." *Windy City Times*. March 8, 2016. Retrieved March 11, 2016 (http://www.windycitymediagroup.com/ lgbt/Second-Wachowski-filmmaker-sibling -comes-out-as-trans-/54509.html).

Baram, Marcus. "Wacky Wachowskis." *New York Post*. May 21, 2003.

Berger, Susan. "*Transparent* Is More than a TV Show, Creator Says: It's Part of a 'Movement'" *Washington Post*. September 21, 2015. Retrieved November 25, 2015 (https://www.washingtonpost.com/lifestyle/style/transparent-is-more-than-a-tv-show-says-emmy-winning-creator-its-part-of-a-movement/2015/09/21/f7d5efd2-5cb3-11e5-8e9e-dce8a2a2a679_story.html).

Bowles, Scott. "Brothers Eschew *Matrix* Hype." *USA TODAY*. May 18, 2003. Retrieved November 10, 2015 (http://usatoday30.usatoday.com/life/movies/news/2003-05-18-brothers_x.htm).

Fierman, Daniel. "Caught in the Matrix." *Entertainment Weekly*. April 18, 2003. Retrieved December 23, 2015 (http://www.ew.com/article/2003/04/18/caught-matrix).

Fleming, Michael. "Sibs Built for *Speed*." *Variety*. November 1, 2006. Retrieved November 17, 2015 (http://variety.com/2006/digital/markets-festivals/sibs-built-for-speed-1117953047/).

Grinberg, Emanuella. "Bathroom Access for Transgender Teen Divides Town." CNN. September 5, 2015. Retrieved October 16, 2015 (http://www.cnn.com/2015/09/03/living/missouri-transgender-teen-feat/).

Heffernan, Dani. "Interview: GLAAD Talks to Actress and *Sense8* Star Jamie Clayton."

GLAAD. August 3, 2015. Retrieved November 25, 2015 (http://www.glaad.org/blog/interview-glaad-talks-actress-and-sense8-star-jamie-clayton).

Hemon, Aleksandar. "Beyond the Matrix." *The New Yorker*. September 12, 2012. Retrieved October 15, 2015 (http://www.newyorker.com/magazine/2012/09/10/beyond-the-matrix).

Hoad, Phil. "Cloud Atlas: How Hollywood Failed to Put It on the Map." *The Guardian*. February 20, 2013. Retrieved November 19, 2015 (http://www.theguardian.com/film/filmblog/2013/feb/20/cloud-atlas-warner-bros).

Holmes, Thom. *Electronic and Experimental Music: Pioneers in Technology and Composition.* 2nd ed. New York, NY: Routledge, 2002.

Marx, Christy. *The Wachowski Brothers* [*sic*]: *Creators of the Matrix.* New York, NY: Rosen Publishing Group, 2005.

McClintock, Pamela. "Global Box Office: *Jupiter Ascending* Finds Redemption in China." *The Hollywood Reporter*. March 8, 2015. Retrieved November 20, 2015 (http://www.hollywoodreporter.com/news/global-box-office-jupiter-ascending-779980).

Miller, Mark. "Matrix Revelations." *Wired*. November 1, 2003. Retrieved December 23, 2015 (www.wired.com/2003/11/matrix/).

Montes, Euclides. "The *V for Vendetta* Mask: A Political Sign of the Times." *The Guardian*. September 10, 2011. Retrieved November 16, 2015 (http://www.theguardian.com /commentisfree/2011/sep/10/v-for-vendetta -mask).

National Center for Transgender Equality. "About Us." January 29, 2015. Retrieved November 13, 2015 (http://www .transequality.org/about).

Pearson, Ryan. "Wachowskis Hope to Surprise with Next Film." *Yahoo!* October 25, 2013. Retrieved December 23, 2015 (https://www .yahoo.com/movies/s/wachowskis-hope -surprise-next-film-183313417.html).

Rich, Joshua. "*Speed Racer* Crashes at the Box Office." *Entertainment Weekly*. May 12, 2008. Retrieved November 17, 2015 (http:// www.ew.com/article/2008/05/12/speed -racer-crashes-box-office).

Silverman, Stephen M. "*Matrix* Maker's Divorce Gets Even Messier." *People*. May 19, 2004. Retrieved November 2, 2015 (http://www .people.com/people/article/0,,639756,00 .html).

Sullivan, Emmet, and Peter Ranvestel. "The Trans 100 Celebrates Another Year." *Chicago Magazine*. March 30, 2015. Retrieved November 24, 2015 (http://www.chicagomag .com/dining-drinking/March-2015/Trans -100/).

Tan, Avianne. "Meet 1st Openly Transgender Official Working in the White House: Raffi Freedman-Gurspan." ABC News. August 18, 2015. Retrieved November 23, 2015 (http:// abcnews.go.com/US/meet-1st-openly -transgender-official-working-white-house /story?id=33156360).

Wachowski, Lana. "HRC Visibility Award Acceptance Speech." Lecture, HRC's 2012 San Francisco Bay Area Gala Dinner and Silent Auction, Fairmont San Francisco Hotel, San Francisco, October 20, 2012.

Weinraub, Bernard. "Brothers [sic] Unleash the Comic Book of Ideas." *New York Times*. April 4, 1999. Retrieved October 16, 2015 (http:// www.nytimes.com/1999/04/05/movies /brothers-unleash-the-comic-book-of-ideas .html).

INDEX

ABOUT THE AUTHOR

Jeff Mapua has written several biographies on subjects including Hillary Clinton, Sitting Bull, and Ludwig van Beethoven. An avid movie fan, Jeff saw *The Matrix* multiple times at the movie theater, hoping one day that he, too, would know kung fu. Jeff lives in Dallas, Texas, with his wife, Ruby.

PHOTO CREDITS

Cover, p. 1 Dimitrios Kambouris/Getty Images; pp. 4-5 Lester Cohen/WireImage/Getty Images; p. 12 © Paul Rodriguez/ The Orange County Register/ZUMA Press; pp. 16-17 Robert Cohen/ St. Louis Post-Dispatch/AP/Images; pp. 20-21 Courtesy Everett Collection; p. 26 George Pimentel/WireImage/Getty Images; p. 29 Ebet Roberts/Redferns/Getty Images; pp. 30, 33, 34, 46-47 © Moviestore collection Ltd/Alamy Stock Photo; pp. 31, 68, 70-71 © Warner Brothers/courtesy Everett Collection; p. 40 Andreas Rentz/ Getty Images; p. 43 Barry King/WireImage/Getty Images; p. 45 © Pictorial Press Ltd./Alamy Stock Photo; pp. 55, 56-57 © AF Archive/Alamy Stock Photo; pp. 62-63 The Washington Post/Getty Images; pp. 66, 84 Jason Merritt/Getty Images; p. 75 © Photos 12/Alamy Stock Photo; p. 77 Tinseltown/Shutterstock.com; p. 81 Featureflash/Shutterstock.com; pp. 88-89 Murray Close/ © Netflix/Courtesy Everett Collection; cover and interior pages graphic pattern L. Kramer/Shutterstock.com
Designer: Brian Garvey; Photo Researcher: Carina Finn